STROMA

By Roddy Ritchie, Alistair Murray and George Gunn

Published in 2011
by The Islands Book Trust

www.theislandsbooktrust.com

ISBN: 978-1-907443-13-8

Text ©

Format concept by: Roddy Ritchie and Alistair Murray
Typeset and book layout design by: Roddy Ritchie
Cover design by: Roddy Ritchie
Island map illustration by: Roddy Ritchie
Printed and bound by: Martins the Printers, Berwick-upon-Tweed, Northumberland

The Islands Book Trust
Ravenspoint Centre
Kershader
South Lochs
Isle of Lewis
HS2 9QA
Tel: 01851 880737

THE ISLANDS BOOK TRUST – high quality books on island themes in English and Gaelic
Based in Lewis, the Islands Book Trust are a charity committed to furthering understanding and appreciation of the history of Scottish islands in their wider Celtic and Nordic context.

We do this through publishing books, organising talks and conferences, visits, radio broadcasts, research and education on island themes.

For details of membership of the Book Trust, which will keep you in touch with all our publications and other activities, see: **www.theislandsbooktrust.com** or telephone: **01851 880737**.

The Islands Book Trust, Ravenspoint, Kershader, South Lochs
Isle of Lewis, HS2 9QA (01851 880365)

This book is dedicated to the people of Stroma

Photographs by Roddy Ritchie

Prose and Transcripts by Alistair Murray

Poetry by George Gunn

First published in 2011 by: THE ISLANDS BOOK TRUST

www.roddyritchie.co.uk

www.alistairmurray.com

peedie@urbanbothy.fslife.co.uk

ISLAND IN THE STREAM

This is a book about an island that lies in one of the most stunningly beautiful and dangerous seascapes in the world. It doesn't really matter where the island is, what does matter is that the island has a name – Stroma, and that people used to live there.

Long after the last inhabitants had departed we bought passage to Stroma to look for film locations. We met our guide, William Simpson, on a warm, wonderful spring morning, on the deck of his small boat. The smell of diesel lay heavy in the air and we set off with expectation and the sun wheeling low in the sky.

Stroma is less than a mile from the mainland but to get there you must cross fierce tidal bores that still bewilder seasoned mariners. Our local pilot knew where to steer though and as we edged into open water seabirds cried for attention. They were soon forgotten as we focused on the island.

From the distance scattered houses give the impression that Stroma still holds a community. Closer, you start to see the decay. As we passed slowly and silently into a sturdy harbour called the Haven, we felt exhilarated but shocked at the disrepair.

Ashore, modern farm vehicles clashed with much older machinery inside an old sail shed. Were some of these rusting implements dragged from erstwhile wrecks? Was this first contact with a self sufficient life style, once flowered and long gone?

We headed inland aboard a robust, open top vehicle reminding us that Stroma now serves as an isolated sheep farm. Albeit one with roads, houses, church, school and a proud red telephone box. All stand empty and derelict against the weather.

Heading north through Nethertown heather sprayed in our nostrils. We passed a string of east facing crofts looking out onto forgotten fields threading down to the foreshore. Skerries littered the horizon.
We were elated yet humbled by encroaching thoughts.

Roddy, George and Alistair

It was as if we were the last men on earth, desolate, aware now of our own future. Will this be what it's like if we continue to ravish our planet? The consideration made personal as we drove past neat gardens all abandoned with their delicate slate slabs still edging the paths.

We halted in a gap between these old homes. Soon we were heading west on foot towards a hidden wonder and our new realm took on a different aspect. We were no longer on an island balancing on the edge of the world; we were at the centre of everything, intoxicated by a vast sky and enveloping sea.

Beyond, all around, was land. From Dunnet Head, the most northerly mainland point in Britain across to the cliffs of Hoy standing like sentinels. Onto mainland Orkney and, closer by, Swona Island stretching across to South Ronaldsay, then a stroke to the Pentland Skerries and back to Caithness. We were in the eye, contented and safe.

Or were we? A great chasm appeared out of the earth; the Gloup. We edged towards this collapsed sea cave that connects underneath the island to the furious tidal races of the west, the Merry Men of Mey. We walked around it caressing the beauty in its cold Sandstone walls and green, elemental deep before separating to make familiar the landscape.

Much later we stood inside a house overlooking the North Pier, intimate, the box beds still intact. A community had lived here buffeted by storms. Why had they left? Where had they gone? What were they doing now? Their empty houses stand in silent witness to the busy traffic of a major shipping lane while Stroma, deserted, sits astride a tidal energy source second to none.

At the end of our first visit we knew there was a hidden and fascinating story to tell. Epochal events may ebb and flow but it's the small things that really matter. Stroma is a microcosm of humanity's fleeting struggle with the planet and still has huge relevance for how we forge our energy future and our relationship with the environment; a small island, a big story.

STROMA

Sheep Skerries

Swilkie Point

Langaton Point

Lighthouse

Wardie Geo

Bay of Caves

Beach of Langaton

Caves

Geos of Bagwa

Scope o'Camm

Little Gloup

Geo of Nethertown

Pier

Whitehouse

The Gloup

Cave

Subterranean Passage

The Altars

Nethertown

Sgeir Gut

Cave

Back Berry

Rammie Geo

Caves

Mains of Stroma

Hill Row

Red Head

Tree Geo

Button Geo

Meml

Church

Telephone box

Schoolhouse

Broad Geo

Bay of Sluggs

Cairn Hill

Falla Geo

Uppertown

Riff of Hebrigg

Natural Arch

Post Office

Cleman Heads

Cemetery

Scarton Point

Castle Mestag

Harbour

Skerry Geo

Mell Head

Cave

Sandy Geo

The Haven

Castle of Girnieclett

Skerry

Twenty thousand years past Stroma was buried under huge glaciers, groaning as they rumbled slowly north-west over what we now call Caithness and Orkney. Time elapsed and once the ice melted we are fairly sure that the current landmass of Stroma had fully emerged into the sun light around twelve thousand years before present.

Early man followed, hunter gatherers travelling north and west probably entered Orkney across a land bridge from Caithness. No evidence of their existence has been found on Stroma. The dangerous waters of the Pentland Firth came later, embracing and making an island perhaps as late as seven thousand years ago.

The first hint of Stroma man lies in a five thousand year old chambered cairn situated at the northern end of the island. This is contemporaneous with Skara Brae in nearby Orkney and before both Stonehenge and the Pyramids. But these early ghosts are tenuous and we have to jump forward to the Iron Age and the actions of a conqueror to define a sense of location.

In 84BC Agricola the Roman defeated a federation of local Caledonian tribes at the battle of Mons Graupius somewhere in central Scotland. Afterwards, he ordered a fleet to sail around the northern limits of Britain to prove it was an island. They would have passed Stroma, inferred seventy years later in Ptolemy's famous World Map.

These were the days of Celtic warrior societies. Their great round stone towers or Brochs are conspicuous around the northern Atlantic seaboard. Surprisingly, none have been clearly identified in Stroma. Early testimony perhaps to the hazards of landing or leaving an island that is surrounded by turbulent currents?

Years rolled by, Stroma and native Picts alike obscured. Then almost nine centuries after the death of the White Christ came the Vikings. Honed raiders, they named the island Straumey; island in the stream, an avowal of its treacherous and all encompassing rips and eddies.

These invaders settled. Their Orkneyinga Saga regales us with tales of Sven Asleifson, the last great eleventh century Viking who hid on Stroma during one of his many adventures. Mentioned too is the Swelkie, a tumultuous devil of a whirlpool to the north-west, the undoing of many ships. The first recorded loss belonged to King Haakon of Norway, foundering on a return north from the Battle of Largs in 1263.

Stroma is about two miles long and one mile broad, built up of weathered Old Red Sandstone sediments laid down almost four hundred million years ago in a fresh water lake and river environment. The rocks have been displaced along a fault line which roughly parallels the road running from Uppertown to Nethertown.

This may partly explain why the eastern and southern parts of Stroma have sufficient coverings of fertile clay fed by minerals in the bedrock, whilst the western side contains considerably more unfavourable and boggy ground. Highlighted by old run rig field patterns the division is admirably enforced today by an unremitting salt spray that floats over the western cliffs.

Common coastal features are Geo's or Goe's, sea inlets, often steep sided and derived from the Old Norse word gjá. Inland, the vegetation is hardy, similar to nearby Caithness, with grasses, heather and small flowers. Noticeably there are no trees, whilst sheep and seals are plentiful on the uninhabited island. The latter are sometimes seen inland during breeding season along with myriads of birds who make their homes on Stroma, including terns, guillemots, fulmars, and eider ducks.

Given the perilous currents surrounding Stroma it is unlikely that the bears and wolves which prowled Scottish forests in the Middle Ages ever made it to the island. But according to legend dangerous wildlife did exist. To settle an ancient dispute for island ownership, venomous animals from Stroma, possibly snakes, were transported to Caithness and Orkney. The outcome was that they died on Orkney but survived in Caithness, of which Stroma is still a part of today.

In 1266, at the Treaty of Perth, Norway officially acknowledged Caithness as belonging to Scotland and ceded the area to King Alexander III. As the medieval period unfolded Stroma is mentioned in 1455 when the Bishop of Caithness granted the castles of Scrabster and Skibo, along with the lands of Wick, Alterwall, Stroma and Dorrery, to his brother Gilbert Mudy.

These were turbulent times and land much fought after. Stroma now passed into the ownership of the powerful Sinclair Earls of Caithness. The island became part of the parish of Canisby, and it is from the records of the church there that ordinary people from Stroma begin to illuminate the pages of history. Unfortunately, during the seventeenth century this was often for individual acts of anti-social behaviour such as unruly conduct or even witchcraft!

In 1659 some property on Stroma was granted to John Kennedy of Kenmuck in Aberdeenshire. Allegedly, Kennedy had killed an opponent in a fight before heading, or fleeing, north. But this new resident soon became active in local affairs and built a family mausoleum that now stands derelict on the south east corner of the island.

At this time there were no active churches on Stroma and people had to travel to the mainland to hear a service. For the majority of island tenants farm life centred on agricultural processes. Crops grown would have included oats and bere, a primitive form of barley tolerant of cool temperatures and a short growing season. Much of the harvests were used to pay rents and life was probably harsh. Common Stroma surnames from the late seventeenth and early eighteenth centuries include Bower, Lyell, Manson, Rosie and Tennent.

As the eighteenth and nineteenth centuries rolled inexorably into the twentieth, the inhabitants of Stroma maintained a lifestyle of great self resilience. Crofter fishermen, surrounded by their fearsome Firth, they worked the land and took from the water. They built their own homes and boats, produced most of their own food and repaired anything that broke.

The main sea based activities were line and lobster fishing. Hand lines were used to catch cod throughout the year, even in mighty winter swells. The men had lengths of lines with heavy weights and a metal rod or sprool attached at one end. From this hung a short length of hemp and hook, usually baited with limpets. When out fishing the boats had to be held still by the rowers, more often than not requiring exceptional seamanship amongst the strong eddies and tides.

Between Spring and Autumn lobster creels were 'shot' off Dunnet Head, Swona and the Pentland Skerries. These were often supplemented by coastal catches around Stroma itself using poles and bags. This hard won bounty was sometimes plentiful and it wasn't unusual for Stroma hard fish and lobsters to find their way into distant markets such as Billingsgate in London.

Average croft sizes were around 10 acres and families usually kept a few cows, sheep and hens with a single horse and pig. Common crops included oats, potatoes, hay and turnips. Water was obtained from wells and horses provided power for ploughing and carrying sheaves to the mill. Men, women and older children all helped in the fields and everything was used in some way, islanders even making their own milk and butter.

Entertainment was also home grown and concerts, sketch plays and dances were a regular occurrence. A favourite time was Christmas, when everyone would gather in the school to see treats handed out to the children while unfortunate pigs were fattened for once a year feasts. But self sufficiency came at a price. The all encompassing sea currents made some feats, such as moving animals on boats to market, problematic. And with no doctor on Stroma, for anyone who was sick stormy weather could prove fatal.

People were leaving Stroma in the early twentieth century. Large families didn't have room to cater for everyone and some men never returned after World War One. A school roll of a few hundred had been reduced to less than fifty by the onset of World War Two.

More people started departing at this time, driven by a combination of lack of work and modern amenities. Stroma had no running water or electricity, wells and lamps serving most of the islanders as they always had done until gas arrived in the 1950's. There wasn't a safe harbour either, boat landings were open and exposed to the angry sea, a regular communication barrier that could be emotionally fraught for families that were parted.

The drift continued, enhanced by ex islanders returning on holiday with growing experiences of other places and, for some, a perception of wearing better types of clothes. In the early 1950's the situation was so acute that a new harbour was built to try and stem the tide. This was not to be. A myth that the exodus was accelerated by money placed in local people's pockets from building the harbour was only ever that. The abandonment of Stroma was underpinned by a growing distance from markets and a lack of employment opportunities.

These are classic migration symptoms and there is a powerful argument that the depopulation was exacerbated by a low degree of Council service provision. It is interesting to speculate whether Stroma might be inhabited yet if it had belonged to Orkney, where a different degree of island support existed. In the end, what keeps communities together is a sense of future. This ended on Stroma in 1962 when the last inhabitants left.

Helen Adams

My home was on the west side. As a child I didn't appreciate the freedom and safety I had in my island playground. Although our food resources were somewhat limited, my mother could always provide a feast and my granny often talked about islanders' innovations. My father's aunt had earthenware hot water bottles, but we weren't as sophisticated. But mum used big, flat, round pebbles from the beach. She would heat one in the oven and wrap it in paper – so my bed was always warm!

I was born in 1935. During the war I remember the bombing of Scapa Flow when all the dishes rattled in the dresser. I was terrified of the airplanes and nowadays my mode of travel excludes these flying machines! I was an only child, as was my father, a crofter fisherman. He also repaired boats which were sometimes hauled up to the end of our house. My maternal grandfather was a lovely man with a jovial nature. I often played tricks on him. When he crossed the Pentland Firth I stuck postage stamps on his wellies because I was 'posting' him to Huna – overseas really!

Our entertainment varied. We had plays, known locally as sketches, held in the larger end of the school. Christmas treats were held there too, always with a real Christmas tree. When I was eleven I had to leave home to go to school in Wick. I can still see my mother's face as she packed my case. It was as though I was going to the other side of the world.

I'll never forget Stroma. I am so proud to be an islander. Even today I still do many of the things my mother did – her style of cooking and baking and her method's of general housework. 'Quoyloo' Stroma was my birthplace where I grew up as a child. I had a very happy childhood and 'Quoyloo' Wick, my present home, reverberates with memories of someone fortunate enough to belong to that idyllic island in the stream.

Stroma memories, enhanced by nostalgia, evoke in me a feeling of youth and most certainly restore my soul.

An island of black fires & memories

houses like open empty graves

photographs & images of the day before yesterday

they fill books & hang in museums

or in the abandoned houses themselves

fading like the reason the people left

above fireplaces or beside box-beds

or submerging into the dust of each year

like the farm machinery into the ground

the yawls pulled high above the tide

passing through the firth of each Winter

to the island of shadows beneath the moss

a spoon found on a beach

a school book forgotten in a loft

how to approach this sea-plate of a place?

Stroma sits like a whale

a salt hill

an eye

the Inner Sound of the Pentland Firth

ripples blue green grey

terns swoop from the sky to nothing

like eyebrows

their trilling screams cut across the Firth

their fork tails follow them

as do the eyes of tourists

seals

poets

The Boy James sails out
Willie Simpson at the helm
a whorl of engines & fag reek
Dougie Fulton sucking the insides
out of a roll up
all nervous energy & boilersuit
conversation wafts across the water

puffins & green tyse cormorants
guillemots & razorbills
all hug the wave crests

Our father was one of three lighthouse keepers on Stroma. When we went there, there were no other children living at the lighthouse. I was 6 and you were 3 and I remember you following me to school so you could go too. Well, I didn't want to be on my own all day. I remember falling asleep on one of the broad window sills in the class room!

The keepers had to make sure that everything at the lighthouse was working properly. Everything was brass. Even the handrail going up the stairs to the top of the tower, and when we went up with Dad to light the lantern he'd shout 'Don't touch the brass'. I remember the gales in the winter time. The wind used to circle round the tower making such a noise, all you could hear was the wind. There was one year we had a Burns supper and one of the keepers was a great Burns man and he recited Tam O'Shanter. Yes, and Dad played tunes on his chanter.

And there were regular dances and whist drives and the like held in the hall beside the school. We would all go there on our bikes. We had no lights remember, but we had a torch and we followed Dad who had Mother sitting on the crossbar of his bike. She never learned to ride a bike. Mother was a hairdresser before she got married and if asked, would cut the other keepers' hair.

Remember when we all used to go fishing, mum, dad and dog and cat too. We both had fishing rods. Remember too the lovely summers. Sometimes everyone at the lighthouse would put food into the wheelbarrow and we would all go along the rocks to the bottom of the cliffs and have a picnic. The frying pan came too and we would collect seagulls' eggs and have a feast.

Great memories, we realised that when we went to the 'Stroma Gatherings' and friendships were rekindled. As lighthouse girls, 7 years was a long time to be stationed in one place. And it was a very impressionable time for us too. We have such happy memories of our time on Stroma and would so love to go back again. Oh yes.

All hail The Gloup

the sunken belly of Stroma

sheer red cliffs & a green moss moustache of a rim

oyster catchers toot nervous for their nests

a couple of lazy seals

relax in the high tide's pool

The Gloup surrounded by bog cotton sunlight

a light so high & deep

it pours like a chorus of whisky

from both rock & sea

the faces of two hundred seals
look up to Langaton Point
all black helmets & nose
fulmars arc above their majestic heads
skarfs paddle onto rocks
& look back out to sea

The Swelkie offers up its salt-mill music

puffins perch before their ledge-burrows

admire their own orange feet

across the Firth the ferry cuts to Gills

two hundred pairs of eyes look to the top of the cliff

where sea pinks & rock daisies

sing their own song of skylark & wren

as the tide drops the seals haul themselves

up onto flagstone ledges

black slug-liquorice arch noise makers

a tanker lumbers through the Outer Sound

like a moving skerray

the seals ignore it

north of the lighthouse the Atlantic and the North Sea

grind the two enchanted quernstones

which are turned by two giantesses

who sing of their love for the Viking Mysinger

who killed Forde the King of Denmark

his murdered blood boils the sea

the two she-giants rise up

the world falls into The Swelkie

& becomes a barrel

a plank of wood

a salt mosaic

of words

sucked down

Margaret Green

I remember my first day at school, walking through the fields. There were no tarmac roads on Stroma. We kept two cows, a horse and some sheep. When I left school I did croft work, like haymaking. You cut it with a scythe, turned it over and built coles. And we had our own entertainment, concerts and the school picnic. There were enough islanders then to have a good dance.

A big shipwreck happened in 1942 when the blackouts were on. We put up a big shelter and me and my sister ran back and forth all night with flasks of hot tea for the sailors. I remember four of them came up to our house to get more kettles on. We put them on the stove and the chimney went up! What a night.

The first time I left Stroma I was taken to Wick. At Huna I was told to wait for the bus. But I didn't know what the bus looked like. We went to Wick and another thing was you'd meet a lot of people on the street and nobody stopped and spoke to each other like they did on Stroma. My granny stayed down on the north end and we often went to visit on a Sunday. She had a big family. They all didn't stay on Stroma. Some of the boys were called up in the war and after some didn't come back as there was no work for them.

They said the people left after they got the new harbour built as it gave them enough money to emigrate, but that wasn't the case. People left gradually for work and other things. There was no electricity on Stroma and we didn't know what fruit tasted like because we didn't get fruit until the co-op came after the war. We had no running water and had to carry buckets of water in from the well. You bathed in a washing tub on a Saturday night and you had turnabout in the tub, the cleanest one went in first. My brother was always the last one in!

When I left Stroma the first thing I noticed was that you got your mails at the same time every day. Everything was done by the clock. People ask 'would you go back to Stroma' and I would if I could take my washing machine!

now the fulmar lives in the poet's house

a row of houses like broken teeth

the flagstone coast of Stroma slides into the sea

the creel boat swims a sea of earth

the sky is a sullen acrobat

fifty years of sheep shit where Mrs Simpson polished

the proud cast-iron range is rusted tight

looking into a house of thistles

the nettles grow where the humans trod

rats scuttle behind the skirting boards

the house on the ridge is a house of winds

from East to West they blow

through scullery & box-bed

then from the image-mill of The Swelkie

blown out

into some other Summer

of a horse drawn binder in the corn

two girls & a boy playing before a hay-gilt

two men building a corn scroo

a man clipping a sheep with a set of gangs

potatoes growing in tidy drills

every house a roof

& above each roof

the particular universe

of time & distance

the upturned cart of events

the salt fingers dragging back
under protest these leavings
into The Swelkie once more
then swatted out by the giant sea-trolls
times failure
the skeleton of a binder
rusts into the green harvest of the earth

in the great steading of the sky
a colony of blackback gulls
cry out to Swona & to Ran
the goddess of the sea
cormorants & shags guard the gates
of the Fallie geo
seals sing as the Sun is clouded in
a shutter falling from the East

what were photos once
handsome then & now
backwards into the blackness
of Stroma Mains set in ruins
a pulp fiction of nettles & chiv-blocks
flagstone roofs lie broken like pottery shards
three cart sheds still hold open
the Eastern approaches of the Pentland Firth
the skeletons of harvest-mice
dreaming of Norway

a startled lamb darts through the rushes
its tail flapping behind it like a castanet

the present nests with a fulmar on a chimney pot
the future is the salt ebb tide
running past Scartan Point like a river
a sleek green cargo ship
pushes through the Inner Sound
with silent oil-fired ease
a fulmar with a broken wing
has chosen the burial ground
in which to die
amongst the crofters & fishermen

John Manson

One of my favourite memories is catching lobsters when I was ten years old with Donald Smith, or Dondie as he was better known. He was home from the merchant navy and we'd fished some bait the day before.

We left overland from the Haven and stopped at the shop for some chocolate and lemonade, and to speak to Dondie's sister. Later we arrived at the north end and had to wait for the tide to ebb to get onto the scope of Langaton, a big reef that resembles a pier. Once the tide had ebbed enough we jumped carefully from one big barnacle encrusted clowg to another to gain access to the reef.

You had to tread cautiously or you could lose your footing. Then we baited lobster rings and set them in about a fathom of water half way along the reef in what was called the sound of Langaton. Our rings were made from old bicycle wheels without the spokes and a piece of herring net was tied around the wheel to form a bag about two feet long. A rope with two corks was attached to the ring to float the bridle and a bait line was tied across centre.

Periodically we'd check the rings and if we saw a lobster lying on the bait we'd give the rope an almighty pull, catch the lobster and keep it in shallow rock pool. In between we used a cod head on a short piece of string in shallower water to draw out more lobsters from their holes. One would pull the bait into his hiding place with a claw, then we'd then tug it a bit further from his hole. This went on for over an hour until the lobster was in the open where we gaffed him under the tail.

We left when the flood tide started running north in the sound with six lobsters. On the way back we called on Dondie's uncle and aunt for tea and scones and gave them two lobsters. Later, when I got to my home I was tired after walking and jumping about all afternoon, but what a day to remember when you're ten!

welcome Icelander

off this coast Hakkon the King lost a warship
battle scarred from Largs
now Stroma sits embattled

Ran rises up
quernstones hanging from her ears
salt to fire
her song

the Stoor-worm
the great sea-serpent
is by Ran's right hand
between Stroma & Swona

the living look to the island
but they see no island
only an altar of silence
upon the floor of the sea
the tides rise around it
like rivers of green blood
the North Sea & the Atlantic
the twin oceans of reality
fuse here in this fiction of your life
island of two human millennia
wordless island of ruin
the people have flaked off you like skin
lost in the ever increasing sea
vapours footprints fingers shadows
all gone to the seabed & the shore
south like money or the wild geese
the living are indifferent to the quiet
for not the living or the dead or the unborn
can mark this island with a brand
from the red fire of time's conspiracy
those who look to the island
carry the death of Stroma
upon their shoulders
now the serpent has surrounded the island
the Stoor-worm has bitten its own tail

other shadows form
on the meagre Stroma roads

Sutherland Manson

When I went to Stroma in 1929 I was only two years old. I cannot really remember the crossing, but I know the boat was called 'Diligent'. Later, I had to go to Wick High school, staying at Canisby with my grandmother. Occasionally on a Friday night I would be landed on the east side of the island, clambering over the rocks to reach home.

Leaving school I went to sea. Island life resembled that of a ship in many ways. I was delighted to go to sea. That year too my father transferred to Thrumster. I helped with the flitting. With no furniture our living room looked so bare, just four walls. I never said goodbye to anyone. I did not feel like saying a final goodbye.

On the last trip across I took my bicycle. I remember it lying surrounded by flowerpots, a strange sight indeed. We passed close astern of a trawler heading west. I wished I was aboard her. I'll always remember that. Love of the sea and ships has never left me.

Before my time Stroma fishermen were in great demand as Pentland Firth pilots because of their knowledge of tidal waters. Wrecks on Stroma were more frequent then as navigational aids of today did not exist and many a shipwrecked mariner owed his life to such men's efforts.

My grandfather was a pilot. He told me that if ships had a favouring wind and tide they sometimes just carried on. The men did not know where they would end up, even America. It was a dangerous life.

I miss Stroma and its folk. Stroma was home to me and will always be a place of happy memories.

who comes down the croft road

in his hand made cart

but Donald Banks the Bard of Stroma

he stops & gets off

pats his horse & steps out

into a picture from 1937

the Coronation year

he has a Union Jack in his hand

the butcher's apron worn over countless injustices

such as the one he inhabits

the silent absence

of opium & death in India

where is your battered cheese-cutter now

Doanly of the necessary verses

where are your famous rubber boots?

They are dancing in the endless dream
which you sleep through at Scartan Point
a porpoise in the endless flow
the ebb tide of death

the island reaches up
& spins beneath the Sun
the final metamorphosis
of lived history
into stillness
as the coven of blackbacks
still posses the cliff-geo

who beckons the wrecks here
is it the lighthouse
Ran or the two giantesses
& their salt grinding quern stones?

The hypnotism of tides
a ship full of apples from America
a steel angel
a black horseman of the future
you unloaded her
Stroma
piece by piece
apple by apple
the hoof prints of the Valkyrie
sounding across the island
as the birds sang
& cattle lowed
motorbikes & nylons
for every croft house
a little bit of Pennsylvania
before the photo faded
& was left behind
in a mouse tracked shelf
in 1931

Jimmy Simpson

I remember my schooldays very clearly, the games we played and my classmates. I remember the lighthouse keepers used to shoot the seals. They got a lot of money for the skins which were sent south. This benefited the fishermen by keeping down the seal population. The Stroma people wouldn't shoot the seals. Whether they had a premonition that this was their fore people coming back I don't know?

Local people did fishing and farming, self supporting. You kept your own cow for milk and made your own butter in old fashioned churns. We got our share of turning the handle, a very boring job. All those days are gone now!

There was a bard, Donald Banks, a real character. He was the coffin maker and did an act at concerts. He never came to rehearsals but had always something witty to say. He would pick out the island characters and make recitations to suit the people. There was also a yacht club. The boats were four to five feet for the men, two feet for the boys. In the winter months they had regattas and I got second one year, a great honour. It was Malcolm Robertson that made my boat, and after he left home I never saw him again.

During the First World War people were leaving to join the forces. More people started leaving after the Second World War. My father was one of the first in 1943. My brother came home on leave and the weather was bad. There was no safe harbour then and my brother was marooned in Huna. My father said if he couldn't see his son when he was on leave he would look for a place on the mainland.

When Stroma was advertised for sale I bought it. It's my home and you never forget your home. People asked me 'why are you buying it when everyone is leaving' and I said I'll work it. It hasn't made me a fortune but it gave me a living and I've never regretted it. I never expected to get tenants back, but tidal power has a great future and we may see people on Stroma again.

your eyes never leave Stroma
when you physically leave the island
Stroma moves North
& in the sea as outriders
a scattering of puffins
a jet pass of guillemots
a sudden dance of razorbills

on the deck of the boat
a box of dark kicking lobsters
Caithness edges closer
Duncansby & Dunnet Head
lock arms
reach out
grab you back

FUTURE

We said that Stroma had a fascinating story to tell and we hope that this book has managed to portray, at least in part, some aspects of an island in the stream together with its community, long since dispersed.

We have barely scratched the surface, yet the individual memories are vivid and real. Significantly, they focus on the simple things that really do matter; a happy day fishing for lobsters and being tucked up in bed with hot pebbles from the beach. Together the recollections evoke a lifestyle that was contented, yet unsustainable.

The community on Stroma had forgone its own sense of future well before the final departure in 1962. Every family and family member had a personal reason for leaving. Nonetheless, lurking in the shadows is a hint of regional and national neglect across the first half of the twentieth century.

Whilst political decision makers lurched from one World War to another the inhabitants of Stroma lobbied for a new harbour. This ensemble for change went on from the second decade of the twentieth century to the fifth. Only then did a new pier arrive, but it was too late. Stroma menfolk regularly braved dangerous currents to enable their children to attend school, or to fetch a doctor. Meantime the adjacent islands of Orkney received a regular boat service courtesy of a neighbouring Council.

The Stroma days glimpsed in this book are gone and won't come back, but the Highlands and Islands still offer a sense of community and quality of life that can be hard to beat elsewhere. The emigration of the Stroma community is a lesson in the fundamental challenge for remote communities; how can we create wealth in these areas to bolster services and hold onto livelihoods?

Since Stroma emptied the world has changed. We live in a faster global economy. Markets are more open and competitors are more international and intense. In general, commercial activities distribute to their most strategic location, and therein lies a ray of hope. Stroma is surrounded by a unique marine resource. One that Scotland's First Minister, Alex Salmond, even proposed in 2010 could make Scotland the "Saudi Arabia of marine power".

This fortuitous circumstance affords an opportunity for Stroma's hinterland to develop new, related enterprises that might grow and export their wares. A scenario that can create wealth by bringing in revenues which can domino demand for local support networks. So let us offer a definition that matters; economy comes from a Greek word meaning 'one who manages a household'.

Economics is basically a description of how goods and services are exchanged amongst a community. This latter aspect is vital. Not just because individuals need jobs, homes and something to look forward to such as culture and the arts. The community itself requires a sense of future. Without a community vision young people will not remain or return to share in something that is exciting. Without an expectation of decent prospects people will drift apart.

In these early days of energy development from the sea, support from regional and national governments must be balanced to benefit local initiatives as well as larger international concerns. Smaller businesses are a seedbed for innovation and community development. Yet patience is required, for the majority of small start-ups fail. This carries an attached stigma and the stark reality is that it is people with hopes and dreams who suffer the tragic consequences; individuals who are more often than not significant drivers within their local communities, the ones that set out visions for the future.

This brings us full circle to Stroma. As we got to know the ex islanders some things stood out; they were proud, hard working and self reliant. This was not enough to save their community and herein lies a salutary lesson. A work ethic exists still amongst the grandsons and granddaughters of Stroma. From this generation local leaders could emerge to take up the new energy challenge, and this time they will need genuine support if their area is not to end up just as a holiday resort for the well off.

Many Scottish island communities have died or faded away, but few have the chance to be reborn, albeit in a different sense. Ancient secrets, Vikings, whirlpools, shipwrecks, exodus: Stroma has been central to them all. Now new hope offers a chance to project Stroma into a different future.

We wish it well.

Whilst working on this book we found the following surnames associated with Stroma over the centuries. Those that are highlighted in bold are the names of the last known croft holders taken from a re-produced map by Donald Young, who had used an original map drawn by William J. Sinclair with croft holder names supplied by Pat Simpson:

Allan	Dunnet	Macaughey	**Robertson**
Andrew	Geddes	Macculloch	Roman
Anderson	Gibson	Mackay	Rosie
Bain	Gills	Mackenzie	Shearer
Banks	**Green**	Macleod	Stephen
Barnetson	Halcro	Macpherson	Steven
Beg	Ham	**Manson**	**Simpson**
Bowar	Henderson	Mathieson	**Sinclair**
Bower	Hunter	Mclardy	**Smith**
Bremner	Inkster	Miller	Sutherland
Brown	Kennedy	**Moodey**	Tait
Bruce	Kersey	**Moodie**	Taylor
Caldell	Laird	Moir	Tenent
Calder	Larnach	More	Tennent
Coghill	Lawson	Mowat	Thomson
Cormack	Leith	Mudy	Todd
Corrigall	Linklater	Murison	Watson
Crockett	Lyall	Murray	Wards
Crowe	Lyell	**Norquay**	**Wares**
Dundas	Liell	Reid	Youngson

THE PHOTOGRAPHER

Photographs help you remember. They act as memories to loved ones and places that no longer exist. They serve as souvenirs of travels, adventures and good times. They also relate histories, detail relationships with other cultures and record rituals, customs and important events. What you chose to photograph and the photographs you chose to keep reflects what you value. In the same way, photographs as shared cultural memories are powerful reminders of what society values.

The above paragraph greets you as you enter the photography section of the Art Gallery of Ontario (AGO) "Connecting with Photography exhibition 2009". It sums up so eloquently what photography, as an art form is all about, and in many ways what this book is about.

Stroma no longer exists as it did. Stroma is a micro example of Scotland's depopulation over the last two centuries. It is a beautiful, haunting island with the voices of its former inhabitants still palpable in its strange and empty landscape. Most of the islanders' homes are derelict, but some still have touching mementos and artefacts of their former lives.

What I've photographed is the decaying remnants of a scattered community that lived in a world of their own. It's evidence and a souvenir of travels, adventures and good times the three of us had on a glorious spring day on a deserted island in Caithness.

I photograph people and places that have stories to tell and things that are important to me. And I hope that the images will serve as a cultural reminder of what society should value in a shrinking world that seems to be culturally at one another's throats.

I've no doubt that the birds of Stroma will hear the sound of laughing children playing in the spring grass again, but when that will be, could be anyone's guess. Stroma awaits patiently the next chapter in her long and beautiful life.

Roddy Ritchie

Photographic equipment: Canon 20D, Canon 5DII, Canon L series lenses.

THANKS

The authors wish to sincerely thank the following people for their help in producing this book:

Helen Adams (née Green)

Dougie Fulton

Margaret Green (née Sinclair)

Katie Herriot (née Ord)

John Manson

Sutherland Manson

Debbie Miller (Photography of the three adventurers)

Jane Murray (Proofreading)

Carolyn Ritchie

Jean Robertson

Christine Russell

Ruth Sim (née Ord)

Jimmy Simpson

William Simpson

Furthermore, a special book on Stroma was compiled and edited by Donald Young in 1992, and we are grateful for this wonderful source material. For those readers who would like to know more about Stroma it is well worth a read:

Stroma, ISBN 1871704073, edited by Donald Young, ©1992 North of Scotland Newspapers

Roddy Ritchie was born in Stonehaven and brought up in the fishing village of Gourdon. At the age of eighteen he ran away to the Advertising Industry. He has a lifetime of experience in creative work provision, design and corporate film making. He now lives in Muir of Ord, where he devotes his free time to photography, painting, astronomy and his hens.

Alistair Murray was born in Banffshire and settled in Caithness after a varied career spanning three continents and ranging from oil exploration to running manufacturing and multimedia companies. He now pursues a number of writing and screen interests and is the co-author of "On the trail of the real Macbeth, King of Alba" (Luath Press).

George Gunn is a native of the Parish of Dunnet in Caithness. He has had seven collections of poetry published and has had many stage plays produced, the most recent being "Fields of Barley" by Grey Coast Theatre Company in 2009. He has also written and presented several series for BBC Radio Scotland and Radio 4.

Sheep
Skerries

Swilkie Point

Langaton Point

Lighthouse

Wardie Geo

Bay of Caves

Beach of Langaton

Caves

Geos of Bagwa

Scope o'Camm

Little
Gloup

Geo of Nethertown

Pier

Whitehouse

The Gloup

Cave

Sgeir Gut

Subterranean
Passage

The Altars

Nethertown

Cave

Back Berry

Rammie Geo

Caves

Mains of Stroma

Hill Row

Red Head

Tree Geo

Button Geo

Meml

Church

Telephone box

Schoolhouse

Broad Geo

Bay of Sluggs

Cairn Hill

Falla Geo

Uppertown

Natural Arch

Riff of Hebrigg

Cleman
Heads

Post Office

Castle Mestag

Cemetery

Scarton Point

Harbour

Sandy Geo

The
Haven

Skerry Geo

Mell Head

Cave

Castle of
Girnieclett

Skerry

ISLAND IN THE STREAM